WALKS FOL
STEAM RA
IN THE SOUTHERN COUNTIES
OF ENGLAND

by ALAN CHARLES

The author's profit from the sale of this book will be donated
to the Railway Children charity – in its fight for the
care and protection of street children.

ISBN 978 1 84674 395 5

Countryside Books
3 Catherine Road
Newbury, Berkshire

To view our complete range of books,
please visit us at
www.countrysidebooks.co.uk

Designed and Typeset by KT Designs, St Helens
Produced through The Letterworks Ltd, Reading
Printed by Holywell Press, Oxford

Contents

Area Map

Severn Valley Railway
● BIRMINGHAM
Nene Valley Railway
● CAMBRIDGE
Gloucestershire Warwickshire Railway
Epping Ongar Railway
● OXFORD
Chinnor and Princes Risborough Railway
● LONDON
● BRISTOL
GUILDFORD
Spar Valley Railway
Kent & East Sussex Railway
● DOVER
West Somerset Railway
Watercress Line
Bluebell Railway
Romney, Hythe & Dymchurch Railway
● SOUTHAMPTON

Map symbols

FB Footbridge

Ⓟ Car park

▯ Public house

❸ Paragraph numbers – linking the map to the text

_ _ _ _ Route of the described walk

_ _ _ _ Other paths, tracks and drives

╟┼┼┼●┼┼╢ Railway lines and stations

✝ Church

■ Other buildings

🌲 Trees

The maps contain Ordnance Survey data
© Crown copyright and database right 2013

Introduction

Although most of us regret the impact that Dr Beeching's Axe had on railways in the 1960s, its effect was not all negative. Had not the closures occurred to the extent that they did, the many heritage railways that we cherish today might well have been modernised using electrical or diesel traction, coloured light signalling and updated buildings. Of course that is good in itself, but we may have lost for ever the old-world atmosphere that today's heritage railways seek to recreate.

It is for those who enjoy both walking in the countryside and visiting these railways that this book is written. Each walk follows the chosen railway as closely as possible while using public rights of way or permissive paths. The opportunity this gives for watching and photographing trains should be welcomed by those who feel restricted by like-minded enthusiasts obstructing each other on station platforms!

It is assumed that you will travel on the railway at the outset, then walk back following the book's directions. The risk of missing the last train back is thus avoided, which might otherwise be the case if the walk came first. However, you may on occasions find it more convenient to walk first; that's ok, as long as you allow plenty of time!

In most cases it is possible to arrive at the railway by public transport, some more easily than others. Advice is given for this in each chapter. Many heritage railway stations have their own car parks, and these are usually free of charge. Alternative car parks are suggested where this is thought appropriate.

Since the railways do not as a rule run trains every single day, it is well-worth arming yourself with an up-to-date timetable, either through the post or via the railway's website. Again, advice for this is given in each chapter. As well as timetable information, each railway provides details of special events – which usually occur at weekends – and facilities such as refreshment rooms, picnic areas, bookshops and, perhaps most usefully – toilets. They will also say whether some trains are diesel-hauled, which may not be to your liking!

Railway websites often feature the latest news items: usually good news, but very occasionally bad. For example, it is not unknown for embankments to sustain damage due to adverse weather conditions, necessitating temporary closure of sections of a railway. And so to avoid disappointment, you are well advised to look at the chosen railway's website before setting out.

Many trains offer onboard refreshments, but your journey may be too short for you to enjoy this to the full. And since these railways depend to a great extent on volunteers, which can be in short supply, you may find that refreshments are not available on some trains and stations when you most need them. In any case they cannot be expected at stations after the last train has departed!

It is also worthwhile having the appropriate Ordnance Survey map at your side, just in case you deviate from the described route – by intention or accident! I have on occasions included compass bearings within the text. You may find these helpful; for example where your destination is a stile or gate out-of-sight beyond the brow of a hill. So hopefully you will include a compass in your rucksack when on these walks – which in any case you may find useful when out in the countryside on other occasions.

Finally, I hope you enjoy this opportunity for 'steaming up and walking down' as much as I did!

The Severn Valley Railway – Victoria Bridge.

1
The Nene Valley Railway, Cambridgeshire

5 miles

Taking the train from Wansford to Overton station and walking back.

Useful maps: Ordnance Survey Explorer 227 or Landranger 142.

'City of Peterborough' crosses the river Nene.

Along with many views of the railway, the chief delight on this walk is the lovely River Nene, which accompanies the walk over much of its length. The walk crosses the river, as does the railway, at Lynch Bridge, and follows its course to the lovely area around the Old Mill and windmill tower, Castor. It also crosses the route of the Roman Ermine Street, which runs straight as a die to the site of Durobrivae, an important Roman town nearby; but to the casual passer-by there may be little evidence of it on the ground.

Railway operating days: In addition to school and bank holidays, trains run over most weekends from April to October. A service also operates on weekdays, most often on Wednesdays, and on many days in August – except Mondays and Fridays. A timetable is available from The Nene Valley Railway, Wansford Station, Stibbington, Peterborough, PE8 6LR. ☎ 01780 784444 ⊕ www.nvr.org.uk

Getting there: By road: Wansford station is clearly signposted from the A1 three miles north-west of junction 17 and one mile south-east of the A1/A47 junction. There is a car park at the station. **Grid ref:** TL092980 **Postcode:** PE8 6LR.
By public transport: Those arriving at Peterborough main line station and aiming for Overton railway station could take the daily Citibus route 1 from Queensgate bus station to Ferryview. Alight there and walk forward along the A605 from the Wistow Way/Brimbles Way roundabout to a path on the left signposted to Ferry Meadows. The path follows firstly a river, then turns left alongside a road to Overton station. On returning to Peterborough, wait for the bus on the same side of the road as on your arrival. The less frequent but quicker route X4 will take you to Notcutts garden centre. Turn right out of its drive and go forward into Ham Lane and forward again along a roadside path to the station. Now take care that you complete the walk before the last train back from Wansford! Note that there is no car park at Overton station; but there is one at the country park nearby. Queensgate bus station can be accessed from the main line railway station by walking along Station Road and over the shopping centre's footbridge.

Eating out: Refreshments are available at Overton station and on the trains. Wansford station has an excellently comprehensive café.

Visitor attractions: The railway enthusiast cannot fail to delight in all that **Wansford station** has to offer. Its HQ is there, as is its locomotive works where engines are restored. There is also a model railway, a travelling post office exhibition, and a second-hand bookshop. The magnificent signal box at Wansford was built in 1907 and is one the largest preserved signal boxes still in use. It certainly makes an ideal subject for the railway photographer!
Ferry Meadows Country Park is easily accessed from Overton station. There are numerous paths for walking or cycling in this area of woodland, meadows and lakes. A miniature railway, a café and a shop can also be found there.

The Walk

1 On leaving Overton station, cross the road alongside the level crossing and join the long straight path opposite. This runs parallel with the railway. After ½ mile the first railway bridge (not on our route) provides an excellent vantage point for watching oncoming trains, while an adjacent road moves off to the right. Ignore a path that follows the road and one that crosses slightly left across the grass ahead. That leaves just one wide well-laid path, which soon takes you straight on under a few trees. On emerging from the trees at a crossing, turn left onto a tarmac path and stay with it when it turns right. After 100 yards you have the beautiful **River Nene** below you, and all around the lovely river meadows. And for ardent photographers there is the prospect of a steam train crossing the river!

2 Drop down to the river bank on the left of the railway bridge (from its far side) and continue with the walk, but now alongside the river and on the **Nene Way**. After ¾ mile you will be diverted away from the main arm of the river by following one of its branches, **Back Dike**. Cross a footbridge on the left quite soon and circulate clockwise around a pond, entering a large field as you go. Stay more or less with the right-hand field-edge, while following Back Dike as before. After crossing another footbridge and turning left you will make a close pass of a derelict windmill before meeting the drive to **The Old Mill**, Castor. Dating back to the early 1800s, the windmill went out of use

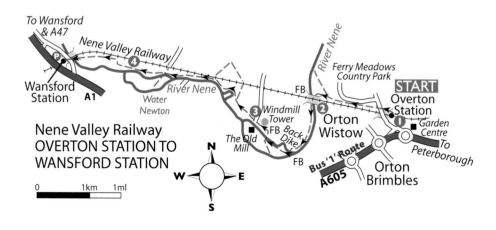

Nene Valley Railway
OVERTON STATION TO
WANSFORD STATION

after 1984. That's a good life-span by any measure!

The Old Mill and windmill tower, Castor.

❸ Go right in the drive and leave it after 75 yards for a footpath on the left. The path appears to divide immediately, but our route is along the right-hand fenced branch, not along the adjacent drive. Soon cross a stile and continue forward (slightly right) with an accompanying dyke on the left and a church spire in view ahead. Turn left with the path and take care on arrival at the next stile (and gap). Here you should ignore the path going straight on and turn left and downhill to a footbridge. Having crossed the footbridge, a branch of the River Nene will soon be close-by on your left – and an excellent panoramic view of the railway to your right. Keep forward now, continuing on the **Nene Way** for 1½ miles while ignoring all branches – even the tempting diversion on the left where a cascading weir (and pylons) come into view.

❹ From here your forward-going field-edge path eventually turns right, passes under power lines and turns left to follow the railway. It's only a short distance now before you are home and dry at **Wansford station**.

Wansford's signal box.

Wansford station's locomotive yard.

The Nene Valley Railway story

This railway is the eastern section of the route which opened from Blisworth via Northampton to Peterborough in 1845. Although the railway was closed down by British Rail in 1972, the seed of preservation had been sown earlier in the form of the Peterborough Railway Society. Part of the present 7½-mile railway was purchased by the Peterborough Development Corporation for the Society's use. The railway reopened from Wansford to Orton Mere in 1977, and to Peterborough in 1986, in which time it had grown from strength to strength. With the exception of the original station building at Wansford – which is destined for other uses – all other stations have either been built from scratch or transferred from elsewhere. In 2007 a short extension from Wansford to Yarwell Junction station was opened. Since this includes a 616-yard unventilated tunnel under the A1, it should offer an interesting, if smoky, experience!

Another interesting aspect of the railway is that it has been modified to the so-called 'Berne' loading gauge, which permits the running of continental locomotives and stock. Through-running of charter excursions from other parts of the UK is also possible thanks to a link – the Fletton Branch – with the East Coast main line at Peterborough.

2
The Severn Valley Railway, Worcestershire and Shropshire – Hampton Loade to Arley
5 miles

Taking the train from Arley to Hampton Loade and walking back.

Useful maps: Ordnance Survey Explorer 218 or Landranger 138.

'British Railways 43106' accompanies the Mercian Way, near Hampton Loade.

The walk initially makes use of the excellent National Cycling Route 45 from Hampton Loade because it closely follows the railway, while enjoying good views of the River Severn. After leaving this cycle trail, the walk follows the riverside path to Highley, where, after a short diversion to the beautifully maintained railway station, continues forward to Arley. An option is to stay with the cycle trail to the Country Park Halt on the railway, and to meet up again with the riverside walkers at the Coal Miners' Bridge.

Railway operating days: With little exception, trains run every weekend from February to December, and every day from May to September and much of December; also during school and public holidays. Trains may not run over the entire railway on some weekends in winter due to necessary maintenance work. A timetable is available from The Severn Railway Station, Bewdley, Worcestershire, DY12 1BG. ☎ 01299 403816. ⊕ www.svr.co.uk

Getting there: By road: Arley, or rather Upper Arley, is best approached from the A442 at Shatterford, 4 miles north-west of Kidderminster. For the station you will need to cross the river by the footbridge. There is a car park at Upper Arley, and another at the station side of the river, but not at the station itself. **Grid ref:** SO764800 **Postcode:** DY12 3NF. Hampton Loade station (at the start of the walk) also has a car park, but it is quite small.

By public transport: Since there are no buses to Arley, your best option is to travel direct to Hampton Loade station (for the start of the walk) from, say, Bridgnorth or Kidderminster Severn Valley Railway stations. The latter has a very convenient connection to London Midland Network Rail services. You will need to make sure that you have time to complete the walk at the very least before the last train back. That's a good reason to have a Severn Valley Railway timetable in your pocket!

Eating out: Hampton Loade and Arley stations have refreshment kiosks, open at weekends and doubtless also during public holidays. And each of the three stations along this walk has a public house nearby. The Arley Riverside Tearooms at Upper Arley (over the footbridge from the station) is open from Tuesday to Sunday until 4pm. So you are spoilt for choice!

Visitor attractions: At Highley station, the magnificent **Engine House Visitor and Education Centre** is home to a reserve collection of locomotives. Along with railway-themed displays and a gift shop, there is a restaurant, picnic area and children's activity area. There is also an admission charge! Likewise the **Arboretum** across the river at Upper Arley, which is open from 10am Wednesday to Sunday and bank holidays, mid-March to mid-November.

The Walk

❶ After leaving Hampton Loade station by way of its car park and joining the road, double back immediately into the **'National Cycling Route 45'** on the right. (had you stayed in the road you would have found the Unicorn Inn and the chain ferry, which was built of wood at the Blists Hill museum).

Along the cycle trail, which hereabouts is called the **Mercian Way**, you will soon be accompanied by the railway line, while enjoying views of the **River Severn**. There are various meanderings and ups and downs in the trail as it passes in and out of the trees, all the while close to the railway.

❷ Hopefully you can judge when you are about one mile from Hampton Loade, for that's when you should stop in your tracks and look for a flight of steps on the left that would normally lead you down towards the river. That is one of two choices you now have (*see below*). The other choice is through a vehicle barrier ahead and coincides with a dip in the trail. The trail rises steeply out of the dip under the trees and in S-bend fashion. Just to confuse you it is now labelled as the **Countryside Trail**! You will have the prospect of a close pass of the railway's **Country Park Halt** along with more views of the railway. Continuing from the halt you would soon arrive at the **Coal Miners' Bridge**. Don't cross the bridge, but wait for us there! (at point 3).

Back to those steps, (the alternative choice) go down them and turn right onto the riverside path, which is labelled as the **Severn Way**. Ignore other branching paths, one of which is the **Poetry Trail**, and keep forward with the river.

❸ The next port of call is the **Coal Miners' Bridge**, where we rejoin those who stayed on the cycle trail. This footbridge was built in 1937 and conveyed miners over the river to Alveley mine beyond the opposite bank. Coal was carried above the bridge by tramway and, later, by an aerial ropeway prior to being loaded into railway wagons on the west side of the river.

If you are on the riverside path, you should walk forward under the bridge and, if you wish, immediately climb the nearby steps to bridge level – where you will find an information board and a signpost giving directions to the **Country Park Halt** and to the country park itself. Returning to the river bank by the lowest path, be here informed

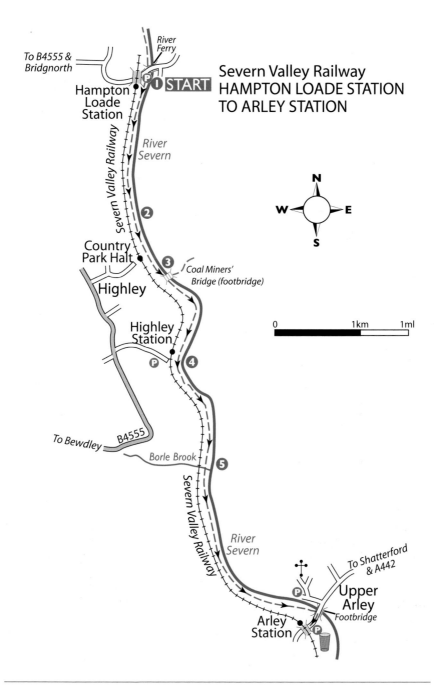

Hampton Loade station.

Arley station.

'Great Western 4566' approaches Hampton Loade alongside the Mercian Way.

that you are on the **Geopark Way**, the **Severn Way** and the **Highley Trail**. Yes, all three! Continuing along the lowest path, soon pass a golf course and, beyond that, a terrace of attractive cottages.

4 You are now close to the fascinating **Highley station**, and a path beside the **Ship Inn** will take you up to it. If you have time to spare, you could cross the footbridge there and visit the renowned **Engine House**, for which an entrance charge is made.

Back down to the riverside path and continuing in your previous direction, soon meet the road opposite the gate to the house Ladymoor. Turning left there into the drive to **Millstone Cottage**, go through a kissing-gate and, after passing a pond, keep straight on through gates and over stiles all the way to **Arley**.

5 On this long final stretch you will cross a footbridge over the **Borle Brook**. This fine piece of ironwork was forged at the famous **Coalbrookdale Works** near **Ironbridge** on the River Severn.

When you meet the Arley road, turn right for the **Harbour Inn** and the railway, left over the footbridge for Upper Arley's car park and the **Riverside Tearooms**, the latter open only until 4pm, unfortunately!

For the **Severn Valley Railway** story, see page 23.

3
The Severn Valley Railway, Worcestershire – Arley to Bewdley

4 ½ miles

Taking the train from Bewdley to Arley and walking back.
Useful maps: Ordnance Survey Explorer 218 or Landranger 138.

On the walk.

From Arley station we cross the Severn footbridge to Upper Arley and walk along the east bank of the river to Bewdley. En-route we enjoy a view of the much-photographed Victoria Railway Bridge and, with a short diversion, the view over Trimpley reservoirs. Another short diversion is to Northwood Halt, an excellent place to watch passing trains and to enjoy a little relaxation.

Getting there: By road: Bewdley is on the B4190, 3 miles east of Kidderminster. For Bewdley station leave the B4190 for the B4195 Stourport Road on the Kidderminster side (that's the north-east side) of the River Severn bridge and soon turn left into Station Road. The station has a large car park. **Grid ref:** SO792753 **Postcode:** DY12 1DU. If this is full, try the free car park in Westbourne Street, prior to Station Road. Failing that, resort to the large not-so-free car park in the town centre on the other side of the river.

By public transport: The Severn Valley Railway station at Kidderminster is adjacent to the National Rail station. The latter connects with Hereford, Birmingham and London (Marylebone). Bewdley is the first stop on the Severn Valley Railway. Bus 125 from Kidderminster bus station runs to Bewdley hourly on Monday to Saturday only. For the bus station turn left out of Kidderminster railway station and walk straight on for ½ mile.

Eating out: Bewdley is well supplied with pubs and restaurants, and the station has an excellent refreshment room. For Arley, see page 13.

Visitor attractions: Bewdley is a fascinating town, as much for its history as for its Georgian attractiveness. Its importance as an inland port and as a manufacturing town in the 17th and 18th centuries is best appreciated by a visit to the **Town Museum**, which is housed in the Old Butchers Shambles off Load Street. It is open daily, Easter until mid-December. Here you will learn about the manufacture of ropes and clay pipes, and about its tanning, brass and pewter industries.

Leave the museum through the rear exit and take delight in the beautiful **Queen Elizabeth II Jubilee Gardens** – or enter the gardens from Lax Lane or the High Street.

The Walk

❶ Cross the road bridge at Arley station and, later, the **River Severn** footbridge. You will have passed – or entered – the **Harbour Inn** on the way. The bridge was opened in 1972 and replaced a ferry which could trace its roots back to the 14th century. Turn right immediately after leaving the footbridge and follow the good path labelled **'Severn Way'** and **'North Worcestershire Path'**.

In due course you will cross a stream on a short footbridge and be steered uphill to the right. You should ignore the branch signposted to Eymore Wood car park that climbs away to your left very soon. As you continue forward you may notice a lesser path running parallel on the right; doubtless this is used to gain a better view of the river or to avoid mud. It eventually joins the main path, beyond which the magnificent **Victoria Railway Bridge** comes into view.

2 I hope you can see from the inscription on the bridge that it was cast, like the small footbridge on the previous walk, by the famous Coalbrookdale Company. Dating back to 1861, and with a span of 200 feet, it was the longest in the world at the time. After passing under the bridge you will eventually meet the steep slope that holds back **Trimpley Reservoir**. You can now take either of the two paths that curve around the base of the reservoir on the river side; but a diversion uphill to the reservoir will reward you with a very fine view indeed, including that of sailing dinghies and wildfowl – and the railway.

3 Back on the path, and making a close pass of the water treatment works, you will see the first of the chalets that grace the riverside from hereon. Many of these were built before the 1940s when planning regulations were not as demanding as they are today.

'Great Western 5164' passes Northwood Halt.

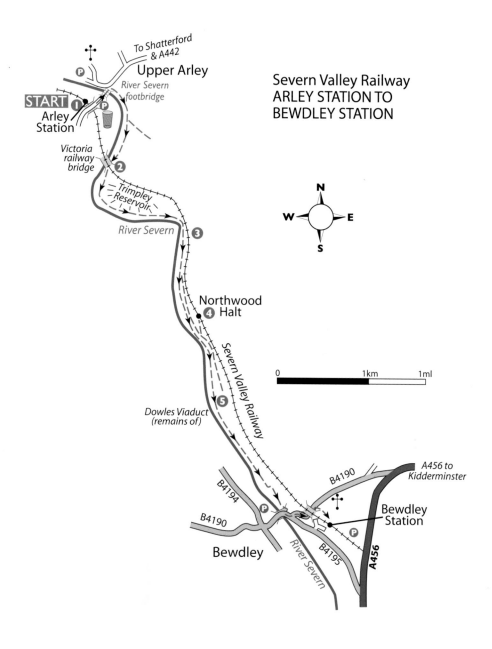

To Shatterford & A442

Upper Arley

River Severn footbridge

START ❶

Arley Station

Victoria railway bridge ❷

Trimpley Reservoir

River Severn ❸

Severn Valley Railway
ARLEY STATION TO
BEWDLEY STATION

N
W　　E
S

Northwood ❹ Halt

Severn Valley Railway

0　　　　　1km　　　　1ml

Dowles Viaduct
(remains of) ❺

B4190

A456 to Kidderminster

B4194

B4190

Bewdley

B4195

River Severn

Bewdley Station

A456

Crossing the river further along is the **Elan pipeline**, which carries water from the Elan reservoir in Wales to Birmingham. Beyond this the path immediately transforms into a tarmac lane – **Northwood Lane**. Ignore a stile on the right at the start (this gives access to many more chalets) and stay in this quiet lane for ½ mile until you meet a branch going left in hairpin fashion. This shortly leads to a level crossing and to the prize-winning **Northwood Halt** – a fine stop-off for viewing trains and for taking a well-earned rest.

4 Return to the lane and continue as before, but only as far as the second shallow dip – by the house **'Bridewell'**. Ignore a rough drive just beyond this and cross a stile on the right almost immediately. This is labelled **'Severn Way'** and leads you in parallel with the drive. After passing a house – the drive's destination – you will be presented with a series of five awkward stiles separating intervening fields, with the river close-by on your right.

5 Coming into view are the impressive piers of **Dowles railway viaduct** which once crossed the river. This carried trains from Tenbury Wells and Woofferton along a line which merged with the Severn Valley line this side of Bewdley. The line was closed in stages from 1961 to 1965.

Next along the path is the curious building and associated contraption that is used to measure water flow on the river; an important consideration with a river that is liable to flooding, as the residents of Bewdley know only too well!

All that remains between here and Bewdley is a lovely wildlife pond and a children's play area. Going left with the main tarmac path soon after this, you will pass **Bewdley Rowing Club** before joining the B4190 road where it leaves the Severn bridge. For the station, go forward in the B4190, and soon follow it around two bends; then join a path between the railway viaduct and the former Red Lion pub. Keep right at the end of this for the station.

The piers of Dowles Viaduct.

Getting-up steam at Bewdley station.

The Severn Valley Railway story

With only four trains a day each way, it's not surprising that this railway along the Severn Valley came under Dr Beeching's spotlight in the 1960s. Although he had his way in 1963, he could hardly have predicted the effect this would have on a group of railway enthusiasts. They came together in 1965 and formed the Severn Valley Railway Society with the object of reopening at least part of this century-old line. Five years later the line from Bridgnorth to Hampton Loade was reopened, extended to Bewdley in 1974, Kidderminster in 1986.

A magnificent new station was opened at Kidderminster in 1986. This was built in a traditional railway style but with modern facilities. Equally magnificent is the older (1861) Victoria Bridge crossing the river to the south of Arley. It is much favoured by photographers and film makers, who wait here for that classic view of locomotives crossing the river. These 'locos' may well have undergone restoration at the railway's Bridgnorth works, with the carriages being cared for at Bewdley or Kidderminster.

One of the railway's greatest assets are the views that passengers enjoy of the river Severn over much of its length from Bewdley to Bridgnorth. Along with this are the attractive flower-bedecked stations at Arley, Highley and Hampton Loade.

This highly successful heritage railway experienced a disastrous setback after the storms of June and July 2007, with no fewer than 45 locations affected, ten seriously. It was up and running again after only nine months. It's a measure of the railway's dedicated staff and members, that they managed to raise the 3½ million pounds necessary to carry out the repairs.

4
The Gloucestershire Warwickshire Railway

3 ½ miles

Taking the train from Toddington to Winchcombe and walking back.

Useful maps: Ordnance Survey Explorer OL45 or Landranger 150.

The 1pm from Toddington heads south.

I t is only minutes into the walk before the magnificent Cotswold Hills come into view, and not long before we meet the popular Cotswold Way. The lovely Hailes Church and the fascinating ruins of Hailes Abbey (National Trust) mark the mid-point of the walk, as does the welcoming sign 'Hayles (yes, Hayles!) Farm Shop, Tea Room and Restaurant'. Views of the railway are enjoyed along much of the walk, but especially so from the field-edge paths along the final mile.

Railway operating days: Trains run every weekend from March to early November inclusive, and, in addition to bank holidays, on certain weekdays from April to October, with a peak of activity from July to August. A timetable is available from The Railway Station, Toddington, Gloucestershire, GL54 5DT. ☎ 01242 621405 ⊕ www.gwsr.com

Getting there: By road: Toddington station is 5 miles south-west of Broadway along the B4632 and 10 miles eastward along the A46 and B4077 from junction 9 of the M5. It is close to the junction of the B4077 and the B4632. Cars can be parked at Toddington station. **Grid ref:** SP050324 **Postcode:** GL54 5DT. There is also a small parking area at Winchcombe station. This station is actually at Greet, one mile north of Winchcombe's town centre. **Grid ref:** SP025298 **Postcode:** GL54 5LD.

By public transport: There is no convenient bus service to Winchcombe or Toddington.

Eating out: The Flag and Whistle is Toddington station's own café: ideal for 'fresh home-made food and drink', but closing at 5pm. Winchcombe station has its own café also, and offers 'scenic railway views' in addition to food and drink! Refreshments are also available on the trains. In Winchcombe village itself there are numerous eating places, including pubs and a fish and chip takeaway. At Hailes, half-way into the walk, there is the welcoming Hayles Tea Room and Restaurant.

Visitor attractions: As headquarters of the railway, **Toddington station** has much of interest, even to those who simply enjoy watching the arrival and departure of steam locomotives. A deeper appreciation is afforded at the station's museum, which is housed in a static coach. A good point from which to view the railway's fleet of steam and heritage diesel locomotives is from the public footpath adjacent to the railway. As fortune has it, this path is the one that terminates our walk from **Winchcombe**. Families would enjoy the play area at Toddington station, and perhaps also the 2-foot narrow-gauge railway which operates on occasional days from April to September. Winchcombe station, where the walk starts, is a 20-minute walk from the town itself, where you can take delight in the narrow streets and old stone-built houses.

The Walk

1 On leaving Winchcombe station, turn right out of **Station Approach**, cross the railway and turn right again – into **Becketts Lane** (Stratford direction). Make your way to the far end of the road where it meets the B4632, using the parallel footpath for part of the way and enjoying fine views of the Cotswold Hills as you go.

Turn right into the B4632, pass under the railway and join a footpath on the left after 30 yards. This soon meets a drive serving a commercial estate. The drive passes to the left of a small car park and connects you to a field-side path (field right, hedge left). Where the field terminates, a large open barn comes into view over to the left and an electricity pole stands nearby. Now take care: the next field takes your path straight on uphill (120 degrees), so don't be tempted into routes that follow the right-hand field edge.

2 Assuming you are on course, you will meet a footbridge at the top, well hidden in the hedge. Keeping forward in the next field, you will very soon meet up with the **Cotswold Way**, which comes in from the right (over your right shoulder, so to speak). Go left with this as it crosses the

'Running round' at Toddington.

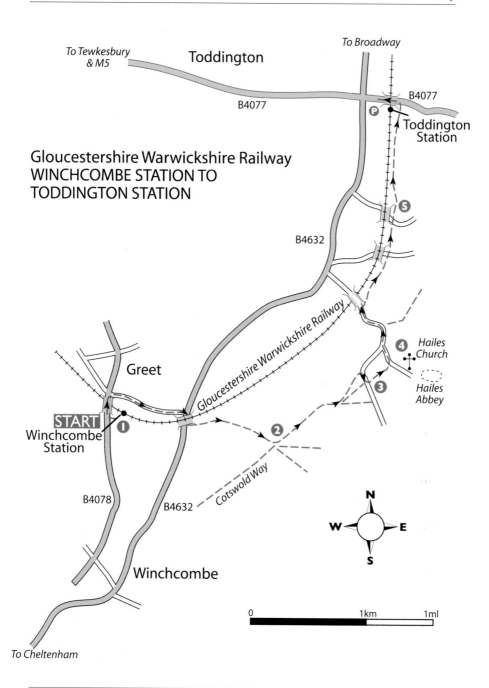

field diagonally (40 degrees), aiming for a knot of trees in the field's furthest corner, where you will find a kissing-gate followed by a stile. Keeping to the same direction, cross the next field and turn half-right when meeting a hedge on the far side. Follow the hedge to a bridleway, from where (if your timing is right) you may see a train passing (distantly) over to your left. Turn left into the bridleway and sharp right into the road at the end – while remaining on the Cotswold Way.

3 Leave the road along a rough drive on the left immediately prior to the first house. The drive serves other houses, including **Pilgrims Cottage**. From a gate at the end, cross a meadow straight on to another gate in the far corner. **Hailes Church**, noted for its medieval wall paintings, is here; and to the right are the ruins of **Hailes Abbey**. Founded in AD 1246, this Cistercian abbey is now owned by the National Trust. Surprisingly perhaps, it is financed and managed by English Heritage, who support an excellent museum close-by. But what may attract your

Hailes Abbey.

attention more than these (initially at least) is the presence of **Hayles Tea Room**!

4 On the move again, go left in the road (if facing the church) and right at the road junction ahead. Follow the road round to the left and look for the footpath sign on the right immediately prior to a railway bridge. Walking parallel with the railway, go over a stile in the far (curving) left-hand corner of the second field. Turn right in the road there and enter a field on the left after 50 yards. Cross to the far side of the field, with the railway still on your left, and join a path under trees. An attractive cruck-framed cottage stands at the far end and a right turn in the road there takes you briefly to a kissing-gate. This is directly opposite the front of the cottage.

5 Following the left-hand edge of a pasture, aim for a footbridge and gate in the far corner; and while aiming for the next corner, notice the very distinct 'ridge and furrow', a reminder of medieval ploughing methods.

'Great Western 5619' departs from Winchcombe.

As you continue forward, the railway's collection of locomotives and other stock come into view, along with **Toddington's signal box**; and a kissing-gate leads you alongside houses to the road. Turn left there for the station and its car park.

The Gloucestershire Warwickshire Railway story

Dating back to the early 1900s, this lively cross-country route linked the town of Bristol to Birmingham. It served the racecourse at Cheltenham and the now popular tourist villages of Broadway and Stratford-upon-Avon. It sported such famous-named trains as 'The Cornishman' and survived a little longer than those that fell victim to Dr Beeching's Axe – until 1977.

Conservationists were there before the event – in 1976 – but not soon enough to prevent the tearing up of all the track between Cheltenham and Broadway. However, they were able to purchase the track-bed in 1981 and were proud possessors of their first operational steam locomotive in 1983. The railway, now the New GWR, was formally opened at Toddington the following year. Winchombe station opened in 1987, Gotherington Halt in 1997. Cheltenham Racecourse station was opened by Her Royal Highness The Princess Royal in 2003, the same year that the railway received the first of two prestigious awards. And now the plans to extend the railway from Toddington to Broadway, a distance of around three miles, have come to fruition.

The railway is run entirely by volunteers. Perhaps the best example of their dedication – and that of their helpful friends from the Mid-Hants railway – is the relaying of track in the 693-yard Greet tunnel in the space of two days in 1988!

5

The West Somerset Railway – Washford to Watchet

2 ½ miles

**Taking the train from Watchet to Washford
and walking back.**

Useful maps: Ordnance Survey Explorer OL9 or Landranger 181.

The classic view from Kentsford Crossing.

The walk follows the **Old Mineral Line** where it runs between the West Somerset Railway and the attractive Washford River. In so doing it enjoys good views of both the river and railway, and the surrounding countryside. A diversion is suggested which crosses adjacent fields from Kentsford railway crossing and heads up to the historic St Decuman's Church and Holy Well.

Railway operating days: The main thrust of the timetable is from April until the end of September, with trains running daily except most Mondays and Fridays in April and September. They also run over most weekends in February, March and December and around Christmas (not 25th and 26th) and the New Year. A timetable is available from: The West Somerset Railway, the Railway Station, Minehead, Somerset, TA24 5BG. Information and enquiry line ☎ 01643 704996 ⊕ www.west-somerset-railway.co.uk

Getting there: By road: Watchet station is on the B3191 approximately 8 miles east of Minehead. **Grid ref:** ST072433 **Postcode:** TA23 0AU. A pay and display car park is adjacent to the station.
By public transport: First Bus 28 to Minehead from Taunton's bus station and main line railway station calls at Watchet and Washford hourly on Monday to Saturday, mostly 1½-hourly on Sundays and public holidays.

Eating out: Watchet is blessed with numerous pubs, cafés and restaurants. Washford Inn is conveniently close to Washford station (at the start of the walk).

Visitor attractions: Washford station was once home to the **Somerset and Dorset Museum Trust**, which commemorated the sadly-departed main line railway from Bath to Bournmouth. **Watchet** is a delightful and historic former harbour town, with two museums and a marina. For lively railway activity, both **Minehead** and **Bishops Lydeard** are worth visiting, although neither are featured on our walks.

The Walk

❶ Go left out of the station and join a footpath on the left labelled **'Old Mineral Line'** just beyond the **Washford Inn**. Completed in 1861, the line was designed to connect the iron ore mines in the Brendon Hills to Watchet Harbour. It lasted on and off until 1910 – well after mining had ceased. Apart from this track-bed, there is little to see of this, apart from **Watchet station house**, now holiday flats, and the goods shed, now a garage. The path soon turns left, then right to follow the backs of private gardens, while the railway runs parallel on the left.

2 On meeting a road go forward into **Huish Lane**, and, when opposite a school, turn left into a cul-de-sac between **Rock Cottage** and **Lilac Cottage**. This is also signed 'Old Mineral Line' and soon comes face to face with a playing field. Go left around the field and soon enjoy views over the **Washford River** – and perhaps that of a passing train.

3 After about one mile (measured from Washford), **Kentsford railway crossing** is a classic vantage point for viewing approaching trains, especially those steaming from Watchet. Not only that but the nearby bench is ideally located for a picnic lunch!

A diversion from the route at this point (described below) would take you, if you so wish, to the **Holy Well** and **St Decuman's Church**. This saint is recorded (according to legend) as having arrived from Wales on a raft, with a cow as companion. The Holy Well is where some of his miraculous healings were demonstrated, including that of rejoining his own severed head to his body. Believe that if you will!

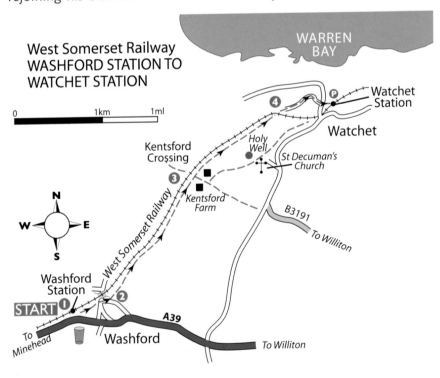

West Somerset Railway
WASHFORD STATION TO
WATCHET STATION

The Ancient Mariner on Watchet's esplanade.

Continuing along the **Old Mineral Line**, you will have sight of the one-time **Watchet Paper Mill** before you pass under a railway bridge. The mill closed in 2015 after 265 years of operation. Depending on the time of your arrival, you may well see 400 homes in its stead!

4 Keep forward (in **Whitehall**) when a road comes in from the right, and stay with it as it crosses the river as **Mill Street** and bears right to become **Anchor Street**. Watchet Railway station is now minutes away.

Diversion from Kentsford Crossing to the Holy Well and St Decuman's Church

From the crossing go down the path on the right and join a way-marked path on the left beyond the buildings of **Kentsford Farm**. Walk the length of the first field and climb the slope in the next, with

The track-bed of the Old Mineral Line.

St Decuman's Church in view directly ahead. Continue climbing beyond a farm gate, but now in a rough track. The entrance to the **Holy Well** is uphill on the left, while the church is nearby at the very top. A right-of-way opposite the churchyard will take you back into **Watchet** and the station – if you so wish. Alternatively return to **Kentsford Crossing** and continue with the described walk.

For the **West Somerset Railway** story, see page 39.

6
The West Somerset Railway – Stogumber to Williton

4 miles

Taking the train from Williton to Stogumber and walking back.

Useful maps: Ordnance Survey Explorer 140 and OL9 or Landranger 181.

The Minehead train approaches Stogumber station.

After following paths and tracks parallel with the railway, the walk encounters the meandering Doniford Stream and the one-time mills that depended on its waters. It joins forces with the Macmillan Way and enters the delightfully peaceful village of Sampford Brett. It crosses the A358 and soon follows field-side paths to Williton, all the while within sight and sound of the railway.

Getting there: By road: Williton station is off the A39, 9 miles east of Minehead. Although there is a car park in the town centre ¾ mile from the station (see below), it may be possible to park nearer the station. **Grid ref:** ST086416 **Postcode:** TA4 4RQ.

By public transport: First Bus 28 to Minehead from Taunton's bus station and main line railway station calls at Williton hourly Monday to Saturday, mostly 1½ hourly on Sundays and public holidays. Williton station is a ¾ mile walk along the A39 and Station Road from Williton's central bus stop – where the shops and car park are situated.

Eating out: Williton has a number of pubs and a fish restaurant. The station itself offers refreshments, as does the delightful station at Stogumber, which is noted for its famous cream teas!

Visitor attractions: Williton station houses a diesel and electric locomotive heritage centre, which is usually open at weekends. For lively railway activity **Minehead** and **Bishops Lydeard** stations are worth visiting, although neither are featured on our walks.

The Walk

❶ Leave **Stogumber station** through the small car park adjacent to the station shop and go under the railway bridge (alternatively go over the railway foot-crossing and descend a short path) turn right immediately from the bridge into a rough drive alongside **Railway House**, with the railway running parallel on the right. Stay with this straight on for ½ mile to **Yard Farm** and a road, passing through a series of gates and over a stream as you go.

❷ Go left into the road and, when it turns left by the house **Bramble Tye**, join a farm track on the right. After a road comes in from the right, cross this to a gate and continue forward, but behind **Cheddermarsh Cottages**. Keeping forward and passing to the right of **Cheddermarsh Farm**, you should follow a left-hand field-edge to the field's far left-hand corner. Once out of the field turn right immediately, just inside woodland and in a level track. The attractive **Doniford Stream** will accompany you under the trees while the following field-edge will lead you to a large one-time mill house, **Curdon Mill**. To your right you have perhaps one of the best views of the **Quantock Hills**.

❸ Turn right prior to **Curdon Mill** and left after 75 yards, passing through a variety of converted buildings to a road, at a bend. Go forward in the road for ¼ mile to where it turns right (for Williton etc). Keep forward here (don't turn right); and when this branch soon turns left keep forward again, between farm buildings and in a farm track.

❹ You are now in the **Macmillan Way**, a 290-mile coast-to-coast walk from Lincolnshire to Dorset which raises funds for cancer support. After about 250 yards leave the track for a kissing-gate on the right alongside a high voltage electricity pylon. Cross the field at right angles to the track to another gate (360 degrees) and, as you do so, hopefully see a steam

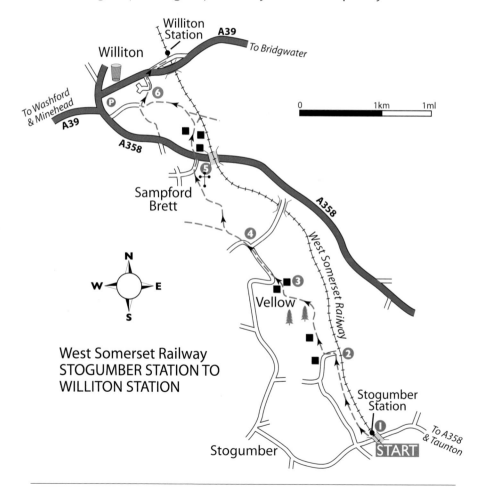

West Somerset Railway
STOGUMBER STATION TO
WILLITON STATION

train passing beyond the houses in the half-right direction. From the gate the path goes half-left and almost immediately right under trees. It passes a waterside cottage and, later, a bungalow. With **Sampford Brett church** coming into view ahead, you will soon be in the village itself.

Stogumber village.

5 Keeping forward from the church, pass two attractive cottages (**'Quarry'** and **'30'**) and in due course meet the A358 road, from where you have a view of the railway bridge to your right. The railway will remain in view after you cross the road to a drive opposite, which passes to the left of a petrol station. This takes you through **Mill Farm** to a stile and gate beyond the farm buildings. Keeping forward in a farm track – which evolves into a footpath – ignore a pedestrian gate on the right and enter a field on the left when the path appears to terminate.

Follow the right-hand edge of what was originally a succession of three fields to a kissing-gate in the far right-hand corner. Turn right from the gate and soon meet a cottage at the termination of a rough drive. Go through a vehicle barrier on the right here and walk alongside a

'Somerset and Dorset Joint Railway 88' from Williton heads south to Stogumber.

field edge. You will soon follow a brook – which is backed by houses – before crossing it and emerging at a road.

❻ Turning right in the road, stay with it until it joins a busier road (the A39). Turn right there and soon left into **Station Road**. Williton Station is directly ahead – where hopefully you will find the café open!

Stogumber station.

The West Somerset Railway story

Standing on the platform at Watchet, you may notice the unusual orientation of the station building – at right angles to the track. The explanation given is that Watchet was, until 1874, the termination of the line. After that time the railway was extended to Minehead, another 8 miles. In 1882 the line was converted from Brunel's gauge of 7 feet, ¼ inch (that's the distance between the rails) to what we now know as the Standard Gauge of 4 feet, 8½ inches. As one of many lines that succumbed to Dr Beeching's Axe, the railway closed in 1970.

It will surprise no-one that a railway in such beautiful English countryside would not be allowed to die. And it was this determination that led to the formation of the 'West Somerset Railway PLC', whose prize was the reopening of the line in 1976.

Fortunately many of the stations have retained their original buildings. Minehead station is very large indeed, with platforms approaching ¼ mile in length. And it possesses a rare structure among heritage railways – a locomotive turntable. This is a fully restored and functioning turntable from the Great Western Railway. At the other end of the spectrum is the delightful little station building at Stogumber, the starting point of Walk 6.

In addition to the many special events that are held throughout the year, the railway is accessible to charter trains which run through from the main line connection at Norton Fitzwarren all the way to Minehead.

7
The Watercress Line, Hampshire

5 miles

Taking the train from Alton to Medstead and Four Marks and walking back.

Useful maps: Ordnance Survey Explorer 132 and 144 or Landranger 186.

Medstead and Four Marks station.

After leaving **Medstead and** Four Marks station, the walk soon enters the magnificent Chawton Park Wood. With the railway running parallel one field-distance away, passing trains may be viewed through gaps in the woodland trees. The path emerges from the trees after two miles, skirts Alton's recreation ground and enters Alton proper. It keeps as close as possible to the railway, enjoying views of it here and there, finally arriving at Alton station.

Railway operating days: Trains are in service over most weekends throughout the year, and on many weekdays from mid-April to September, also around bank and school holiday periods. Bear in mind that diesel-multiple units alternate with steam locomotives during less busy periods. If you inadvertently arrive on non-operating days, there is always the X64 bus to resort to (*see below*). A Watercress Line timetable is available from: Mid-Hants Railway, The Railway Station, Alresford, Hants, SO24 9JG. ☎ 01962 733810 ⊕ www.watercressline.co.uk

Getting there: By road: Alton station is close to Normandy Street (which is the continuation of High Street). The town is bypassed by the A31. There is a large pay and display car park adjacent to Alton station (cheapest at weekends) and a small parking area at Medstead and Four Marks station. **Grid ref:** SU724397 **Postcode:** GU34 2PZ.
By public transport: There is a ½ to 1-hourly train service from London, Waterloo to Alton every day. Stagecoach bus 64 from Winchester bus station to Alton rail station via Four Marks runs hourly Monday to Saturday, 2-hourly Sundays and bank holidays. You could of course alight from the bus at Four Marks (at Station Approach) and start the walk straight away from there.

Eating out: There is a small snack bar on Alton station (open weekdays and Saturday mornings) and a good sit-in café in the adjacent car park. Refreshments are also available at both Alresford and Ropley stations, but these are beyond the scope of our walk today – unless you feel inclined to take an extended ride on the railway! Alton's High Street is well supplied with pubs and restaurants.

Visitor attractions: If you have time in hand, it is worth taking the train all the way to the delightful town of **Alresford**. The mechanically minded could alight at **Ropley** in order to view the engineering works where locomotives and carriages are renovated. Alight on the way back at Medstead and Four Marks for the walk. After all that, a perambulation of the fascinating town of **Alton** must await another day! So might also a visit to **Jane Austen's house** at nearby **Chawton**.

The Walk

1 On leaving the station at Medstead and Four Marks (from the booking office side) cross the small car park to **Stoney Lane** (which indeed it is!) and stay with this as far as the first junction of ways, just prior to a bungalow. Take the right-hand branch here, **Boyneswood Lane**, eventually turning right with it and meeting a road after a further 300 yards. Turn left in the road and leave it when it goes left by the entrance to **Chawton Park Wood**. Join a bridleway on the right here – not into the car park entrance – and immediately pass an electricity sub-station.

2 You now have a magnificent two-mile walk through this wood, initially accompanied by two parallel paths – which may be kinder on your feet than the main path! When the innermost path goes off to the left you should continue forward, preferably along the left-hand of the two remaining paths. With a field now in view on the right, you may have sight or sound of a train passing beyond its far side; or you may need to content yourself with its smoke!

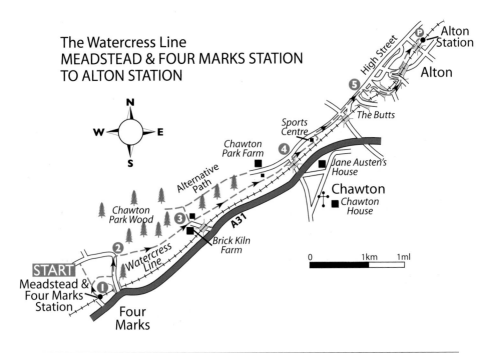

The Watercress Line
MEADSTEAD & FOUR MARKS STATION
TO ALTON STATION

'Lord Nelson' departs from Medstead and Four Marks station.

③ Brick Kiln Farm is your next port of call, where a lane comes in from the right. You could divert steeply down the lane for a closer view of the railway, and then come back. Another option is to avoid what you might consider an intrusion on this walk – a motorcycle trail a little further along in the field over to the right, generally in use at weekends. With this in mind an alternative and attractive route from hereon is described at the end of the walk. This will add ¼ mile to your day. Otherwise continue forward from the farm, soon passing between the woods and a hedge, and with the motorcycle trail on the right. A sloping field will come into view on the left, and you will in due course meet a road at a bend.

④ Turn right in the road and soon join **Cycle Route No. 23**, which follows the right-hand border of **Jubilee Playing Fields**, with the

'Lord Nelson' is ready to depart from Alton station.

railway running parallel on the right. At the far end of the playing fields go left behind the pavilion and soon join the road. Turning right in the road you must now expect the busiest part of the walk; but take heart, this is compensated by a number of crossings of the railway! Stay with the road to a major crossing and continue forward, but now across a large triangular green – **The Butts**. This, as a plinth at the far end explains, was once used for archery practice.

5 Turn right into **Tower Street** just beyond the fire station (or keep straight on if you hanker after the town centre and its shops!). Turn first left out of Tower Street, then right at the end. This will take you past **Alton Baptist Church** and steeply uphill over the railway, where you have another photo opportunity. On arrival at the top of the hill, go left into **New Barn Lane** and left again at the end into **Windmill Hill/Turk Street** – where you have another crossing of the railway.

Go down **Turk Street** and turn right at the bottom of the hill into **Lower Turk Street**. With the **Molson Coors brewery complex** over to your left, join a path just before another (yes, another!) railway bridge. This keeps the complex on your left and is signposted to the railway station. At the far end of the path you will need to turn left in a road and cross to a flight of steps and the station.

Diversion from Brick Kiln Farm
With your back to the farm go along a path to the left of a large house and its garden. This is a left-hand turn with respect to your previous direction. Pass through a gate, re-enter the wood and go straight on downhill to the valley bottom. Turn right into the track there and stay with this for ¼ mile to a gate. Continue forward – initially in a field-side path – towards **Chawton Park Farm**. Beyond the farm a drive takes you straight on, eventually to meet a road, at a bend. Continue from '4' on page 43.

The Watercress Line story
Originally known as the Mid-Hants Railway, the line took on its present less formal name on account of the many watercress beds that existed in the Alresford area. In addition to carrying this delicious product (you may not agree!) and many other local products, the railway was considered as a secondary route to Southampton. It was relieved of this responsibility in 1973, closed down and the track removed. As often happens, railway enthusiasts took on the challenge, reopening the line from Alresford to Ropley four years later. After much voluntary – and muscular – effort, the track was re-laid from Ropley to Four Marks, and opened to traffic in 1983. The next phase took the railway to its final destination – Alton – by 1985.

There is now little chance of the Watercress Line returning to Winchester and the main line now that the M3 motorway has carved its route across the railway's alignment. A level crossing on the motorway would hardly be welcomed!

Two other railways branched out from Butts Junction, one mile south-west of Alton station. These are the Meon Valley Line to Fareham and the Basingstoke and Alton Light Railway. Although these are now long gone, you may be able to trace them on your map – depending on its vintage!

8
The Bluebell Railway, Sussex
5 miles

Taking the train from Horsted Keynes to Kingscote and walking back.

Useful maps: Ordnance Survey Explorer 135 or Landranger 187.

'C-class 592' has just left Sharpthorne tunnel with vintage Metropolitan Line coaches.

The walk enjoys some of the delights of the Sussex Weald, with its great variety of woodland and unspoilt pastures. There are good views of the railway along the way, and, at the half-way point, a welcome (but small) picnic area above Sharpthorne railway tunnel. Rest awhile there and enjoy the familiar sound of steam engines emitted from the nearby ventilation shaft!

Railway operating days: Trains are in service over the entire railway on many weekends throughout the year except during January and November and on many weekdays from early April to October; also on days leading up to Christmas. A timetable is available from Sheffield Park Station, East Sussex, TN22 3QL. ☎ 01825 720800 ⊕ www.bluebell-railway.co.uk

Getting there: By road: Horsted Keynes station is 5 miles north-east of Haywards Heath. Take the B2028 through Lindfield (a most attractive village) followed by one of two roads on the right signposted to Horsted Keynes. Just prior to the village a signpost directs you to the station, where there is a large car park. **Grid ref:** TQ371293 **Postcode:** RH17 7BB.

By public transport: There is a frequent rail service to Haywards Heath from London Victoria and the south coast (Brighton or Hove); also from Bedford, London and Brighton on the Thameslink service. Metrobus 270 from Haywards Heath National Rail station calls at Horsted Keynes station hourly on Saturdays, 2-3 hourly on Sundays. On Monday to Friday the bus calls hourly, but at the village only, which involves a pavement-less road walk of one mile to the station.

Eating out: There is a small refreshment room at Horsted Keynes station, and at Kingscote station. Sheffield Park station (not on our walk but worth visiting) has a restaurant and bar. And needless to say there are platform benches and picnic tables a-plenty throughout the railway for al-fresco dining.
In Sharpthorne (half-way into the walk) you will find the Organic Café at the junction of Top Road with Station Road. But don't look for the station itself, because it's no longer there!

Visitor attractions: These are largely based at **Sheffield Park station** at the southern terminus of the railway. They include a museum, gift shop and model railway. And there is the opportunity to see steam locomotives awaiting restoration. The National Trust's **Sheffield Park Garden** is one mile from the station. None of that is on our walk, but **Horsted Keynes** is; and that's where we find a great deal of old-world railway atmosphere.

The Walk

❶ From Kingscote station go uphill in the road and join the second drive on the left after 200 yards. **Tickeridge Barn** is nearby and a sign introduces **Kingscote Vineyard**. Assuming your timing is right, you will soon have a good photo opportunity through gaps in the trees on the left, since the railway passes close-by. You will now need to keep forward in the main drive for one mile until it turns left by a large timber-clad house, at **Birch Farm**.

2 Leave the drive here and cross the field on the right, diagonally to its far right-hand corner, and join a woodland path. This eventually meets a wide woodland track, where you should turn left. Keep forward in the main track for ¾ mile, until it meets a road at **Sharpthorne**. Here the sight and sound of steam trains heading for **Sharpthorne tunnel** will surely make your day!

3 Moving on again, don't cross the railway, but turn right alongside houses. Follow the road uphill to where it turns left over the tunnel mouth (the longest tunnel in preservation, by the way!) and join a tarmac path on the right between gardens. The ventilation shaft is at the top; and there are seats for that well-earned rest. You are now half-way into the walk.

Continue on the path and turn left on the road through Sharpthorne. (The **Organic Café** is ahead – at the junction of this road with **Station Road**). Leave the road from a point between a small supermarket and **Sharpthorne Club** on the right and join what

START
● ❶ Kingscote Station

Bluebell Railway
KINGSCOTE STATION TO
HORSTED KEYNES STATION

❷
■ *Birch Farm*

N
W — E
S

0   1km   1ml

❸
Sharpthorne

Tunnel ❹

Bluebell Railway

❺

❻

Horsted Keynes Station ❼ P

To B2028 & Haywards Heath

To Horsted Keynes & A275

Ex-Southern Railway '1638' idles at Kingscote station.

is labelled as the **Sussex Border Path**. The path turns left around the clubhouse, passes between hedges and alongside woodland, eventually meeting a field corner.

4 There now follows a sequence of field paths, ultimately meeting a farm drive. Spelling this out in detail: follow the first field-edge to the far left-hand corner and go down the next field to its far right-hand corner, crossing a brook on arrival. Keep right from the crossing and climb the next field diagonally to its upper right-hand corner (190 degrees). After bearing slightly left across the next field (relative to your previous direction), cross another field towards a small brick-built barn in the far right-hand corner and yet another field to its far right-hand corner. Turn left in a drive there – by **Coverdale**, a converted farm building – and right in the 'main' road ahead.

5 Leave the road after about 400 yards and join a signposted path on the right a little beyond the drive to **Vaex End**. This passes close to the garden of **Vox End** and enters a field on the left. Proceed along a succession of field edges (from where there are good views of the railway) and make your exit by a railway bridge. With the colourful semaphore signals just here, and a good view up and down the railway, you have another excellent photo opportunity.

6 Cross the lane here to a field corner and follow the railway to a foot-crossing over the track. Continue forward, but with the railway on your left and until a locked gate bars the way ahead. Join a path on the right here, through a small plantation and into a field. Leave the field after 30 yards and double back over a stile on the left in order to cross the railway bridge. On entering the **Bluebell Railway car park**, keep over to the right and soon arrive at Horsted Keynes station.

The Bluebell Railway story

The railway from East Grinstead to Lewes in Sussex can trace its beginnings to the 1870s as an idea in the minds of local residents and landowners. It came to fruition with the backing of the London, Brighton and South Coast Railway in 1882. While it enjoyed a successful career transporting a variety of local products, it soon set its sights further – to embrace the tourist traffic to the coastal towns of Brighton and Eastbourne. But, by the turn of the century it had become a 'rural backwater'; and with the advent of mechanised road transport in later years it was about to breathe its last. So bad was the situation that the train crew often outnumbered passengers! Although the line finally closed in 1958, conservationists were quick off the

'C-class 592' relaxes at Horsted Keynes.

1957-built '80151' pulls away from Horsted House Farm crossing.

mark. They formed a society in 1959 and obtained a Light Railway Order the following year; and were soon in the proud possession of their first steam locomotive – 'Stepney' – along with access to the section of line between Horsted Keynes and Sheffield Park.

As the very first passenger-carrying standard-gauge railway to be preserved, the Bluebell enjoyed a resounding success, with 92,000 passengers being carried in 1961. With its northern extension from Kingscote to East Grinstead complete, the railway now enjoys a connection to the national railway network. This costly enterprise has involved the clearing of Imberhorne Cutting, which had unfortunately been used as a municipal landfill site.

While you are waiting for a train at Horsted Keynes, you may become aware of a railway track heading off from beyond the signal box. This is the one-time branch to Ardingly, which may in the fullness of time join the ranks of the preserved.

9
The Spa Valley Railway, Tunbridge Wells, Kent

5 miles

Taking the train from Groombridge to Tunbridge Wells and walking back.

Useful maps: Ordnance Survey Explorer 135 or Landranger 188.

'Great Western 7715' from Groombridge is on its way to High Rocks and Tunbridge Wells.

On leaving the Spa Valley station at Tunbridge Wells and the suburbs of the town, the walk enters Friezland Wood. It runs parallel to the railway for ¾ mile, offering views of passing trains through gaps in the trees. The impressive sandstone outcrop, High Rocks, accompanies the path to the road by High Rocks Inn and station. More woodland follows before the path hits open country (with more railway views) and finally approaches Groombridge Place and Groombridge village.

Railway operating days: Trains are scheduled for most weekends from May until October inclusive, and in December for the Santa Specials (except Dec 25th and onwards), also on Thursdays from June to July, and over much of August and early September. A timetable is available from The Spa Valley Railway, West Station, Royal Tunbridge Wells, Kent TN2 5QY. ☎ 01892 537715 ⊕ www.spavalleyrailway.co.uk

Getting there: By road: Groombridge is on the B2110 five miles south-west of Tunbridge Wells. On arrival keep left into Station Road for the village car park. Parking is very limited near the station itself. Access to the station is further uphill on the left. **Grid ref:** TQ532370 **Postcode:** TN3 9RD.

By public transport: Metrobus route 291 from Tunbridge Wells main line station to Crawley calls at Groombridge hourly Monday to Saturday, infrequently on Sundays. If arriving at Tunbridge Wells main line station you could, if you prefer, walk through the town to the Spa Valley station and then to Groombridge as described in the walk details overleaf. But you would want to make sure that you arrive in time for at least the last train back from Groombridge. If you do miss it, you could catch the 291 bus back. The best walking route through Tunbridge Wells from one station to the next is via the Pantiles, a short piece of the A26, and Neville Terrace.

Eating out: There is a buffet at the Spa Valley Railway's Tunbridge Wells West station, and at Groombridge station. These close after the last train of the day has departed. The Junction Inn is located near the station at Groombridge, while the Crown Inn is nearby on the B2110. The High Rocks Inn is adjacent to High Rocks station, the first stop out from Tunbridge Wells.

Visitor attractions: If time allows, do try to walk through the **Pantiles**, a delightful colonnaded shopping area in **Tunbridge Wells**. It is only a five minute walk from the Spa Valley Station. Near the other end of the railway stands the magnificent **Groombridge Place**, with gardens laid out by John Evelyn. The gardens are open to the public, as is the **Enchanted Forest**, which is especially enjoyed by children. The **Spa Valley station** at Tunbridge Wells also has much of interest, including locomotive restoration, an excellent model railway, and a tiny cinema.

The Walk

① From the Spa Valley station at Tunbridge Wells go to the left (with your back to the supermarkets) and into **Neville Terrace**. The original station building (now a restaurant) will be behind you as you make your way to the A26. Turn left there (the Lewes direction) and proceed as far as **Broadwater Lane** on the left. Go along this to a path on the right just beyond the railway bridge. The path passes between the railway embankment and a housing estate and turns left before meeting the A26 at a pedestrian crossing. If you miss the Broadwater Lane turning, you could stay on the A26 and turn left with it to the pedestrian crossing.

② Once over the A26 crossing keep forward in a residents' walkway. Soon turn left, then right after 20 yards between the houses (**Roper's Gate**) and walk alongside the railway embankment (**Spring Walk**). This path emerges into a small parking area before entering **Friezland Wood**, from which there are, from here on, numerous opportunities to view passing trains. After your path (the main path) climbs through the wood, the magnificent **High Rocks** outcrop comes into view.

③ Finally leaving the wood, go forward in the road past the **High Rocks Inn**. You may find the station gate locked, since this is only opened

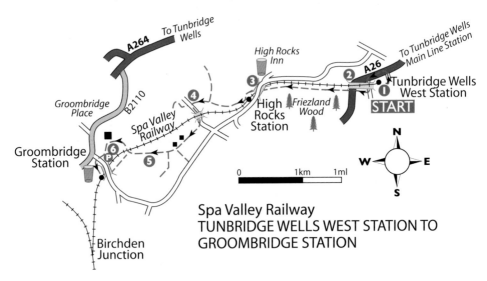

Spa Valley Railway
TUNBRIDGE WELLS WEST STATION TO GROOMBRIDGE STATION

'London Transport L99' prepares to pull away from Groombridge.

after arrival of a train – by the train guard. This is unfortunate, since the platform is an ideal spot for a little relaxation. From the station gate follow the enclosing fence downhill and under the railway; then over a brook and into the path's left-hand turn. Staying with the woodland path you will eventually emerge into an open area of grass and scattered trees – by a magnificent oak tree. Keeping forward awhile you should cross a stile on the right and follow a path to a junction of ways. Turn left here (with the signposted **Link Route**) through a metal gate and uphill in a field. Joining a drive at the top, stay with this as far as a road.

4 We avoid contact with the sewage farm ahead (and much of its odours) by turning left in the road and going down this and over a river bridge. Climbing the ensuing hill, an opening on the right provides a view of the railway, and, if this is your lucky day, that of a passing train.

Continuing on the road, a footpath sign on the right near the top of the hill (when it first levels out) directs you under trees and into a field corner. While enjoying another good view of the railway, cross the field to its far right-hand corner and go forward on a tarmac drive. On arrival amongst farm buildings, turn half-right at a farm crossing and join a path behind a hedge on the left opposite a large stable and open barn. This path, which may not be easy to find, maintains your previous direction and passes a brick-built office building and, on your right, a large pond.

⑤ Now take care: continuing forward from the pond, but just a little to the right, immediately enter a very large and magnificent meadow. Here you will, I am certain, share my delight – and not only on account of a great railway view! Initially following the short left-hand wood edge, go straight on across the meadow, with the railway running parallel well down to your right.

On leaving the meadow from its far extremity, you will walk alongside a line of magnificent oak trees and enter a further field at its corner. A few more paces and you are at a railway underpass and a parting of the ways. If you are bent on returning to **Groombridge** post-haste, you should continue forward, initially alongside woodland, and straight on along a clearly defined path. Otherwise come with me under the railway, along a path and into a field corner. Then with **Groombridge Place** coming into view, follow the left-hand edge of the field followed by an avenue of lime trees.

⑥ Near the first entrance to **Groombridge Place**, go left in the drive for a few yards only and leave it for a path between wire fences. Soon go half-left in the path (part of the **High Weald Walk**) between the fence and a hedge and make your exit into a recreation area. Aim towards the right-hand end of a car park (where you may have left your vehicle) and turn left between this and the village hall. For the railway station turn left in the road; for the bus to **Tunbridge Wells** turn right and go down to the roundabout at the bottom of the hill.

Ex-London Transport locomotive 'L99' at Tunbridge Wells.

A Tunbridge-bound train passes below Friezland Wood.

The Spa Valley Railway story

Once part of the London, Brighton and South Coast Railway, the line from Eridge was opened in 1866 and terminated in an impressive station building at Tunbridge Wells. This still stands, but as a restaurant, and is recognisable by its imposing clock tower. The present Spa Valley station occupies part of the original engine shed. Around 1876 a tunnel was dug between the two Tunbridge Wells stations. This enabled a direct connection between two main lines linking London to the south coast. With more than 100 trains passing each day, the line became a popular cross-country route. But it was not to last. Following the increased dependence on road traffic, eventual closure was inevitable; and this came in 1985.

Enter the Tunbridge Wells and Eridge Railway Preservation Society (TWERPS!), whose penultimate triumph was the line's reopening as far as Groombridge by August 1997. Only one year later an intermediate station was opened at High Rocks. Interestingly this was built by, and on land belonging to, the owner of High Rocks Inn. That's why access to the station is only possible when a train is at the station. The railway's most recent achievement was the extension from Groombridge to Birchden Junction in 2005, and by 2011, to Eridge on the main line between London and the south coast.

Although the railway has achieved its enviable status by the determined efforts of volunteers, encouragement and practical help came from Sainsbury's, whose store lies close to the railway at Tunbridge Wells. Support when it was needed also came from two local councils and from British Rail.

10
The Kent and East Sussex Railway – Rolvenden to Tenterden
3 miles

Taking the train from Tenterden to Rolvenden and walking back.

Useful maps: Ordnance Survey Explorer 125 or Landranger 189.

It's all quiet at Tenterden on a sunny summer's day.

This **easy-going walk enjoys views** across the High Weald Area of Outstanding Natural Beauty, expressed here in a varied landscape of gentle undulating hills, woodland and beautiful meadows. Throughout the walk there are three crossing-points of the railway and excellent views of passing trains.

Railway operating days: Trains are in service over many weekends throughout the year, the exceptions being during the months November, and January to March. They also run on numerous weekdays from April to September and on school and bank holidays. In August the trains run every day. A timetable is available from Tenterden Town Station, Station Road, Tenterden, Kent, TN30 6HE. ☎ 01580 765155 ⊕ www.kesr.org.uk

Getting there: By road: Tenterden is on the A28 road between Ashford and Hastings. Tenterden station has free parking for their passengers. **Grid ref:** TQ882335 **Postcode:** TN30 6HE. There is limited roadside parking opposite Rolvenden station.

By public transport: Arriva bus route 12 from Maidstone to Tenterden via Headcorn railway station runs hourly Monday to Saturday, 1½ hourly Sunday. Tenterden station is located in Station Road (not surprisingly), which is off the High Street from the Vine Inn.

Eating out: Tenterden station refreshment rooms (formerly a motor services waiting room in Maidstone) serves 'a range of traditional favourites' on railway operating days. Refreshments are also available on the trains. There are numerous pubs and cafés in the town itself.

Visitor attractions: An award-winning **museum** at **Tenterden station** commemorates the railway's founder, Colonel Stephens, and the **museum** in Station Road charts the history of **Tenterden**. A heritage trail leaflet for this delightful town is available from the Tourist Information Centre in the High Street. At **Rolvenden station**, where the walk starts, a public gallery affords a truly atmospheric view of the locomotive yard.

The locomotive depot at Rolvenden station.

The Walk

❶ Turn right out of Rolvenden station into the A28 and join a farm track on the left after 50 yards. This is described as a Restricted Byway and leads to **New Barn Farm**. It takes you firstly across the railway and then uphill to the farm itself. Looking back as you ascend, you have a great view of the railway as it sweeps its way round to the station.

❷ On arrival at the farmyard turn right in hairpin fashion and enter a field on the right, aiming for an exit near the far extremity of a wood. Keep straight on and downhill in the next two fields, passing through an intermediate gate in the process and meeting two stiles and a footbridge in the far left-hand corner. Once in the next field walk parallel with the railway embankment (which will be on your right) and make your way to another footbridge.

❸ Turn right to cross the footbridge, and very soon the railway line. Turn left from the railway and soon go over a stile and into a field corner. Once over that stile you should cross the next field uphill and roughly half-right (110-120 degrees). If you aim slightly left of the barns ahead – which will soon come into view – you will be more or

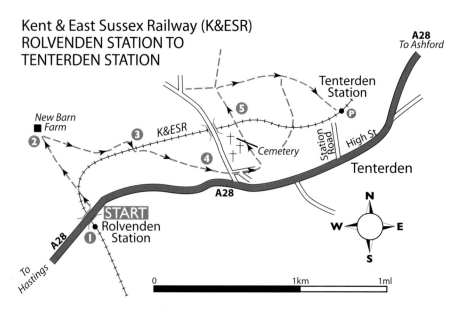

Kent & East Sussex Railway (K&ESR)
ROLVENDEN STATION TO
TENTERDEN STATION

less on the correct course. Cross a stile over to the left of the barns and continue in the same direction as before (half-right with respect to the stile) but now in a very large field, and with the railway in view down to your left.

4 You should arrive at a road about 50 yards to the left of its junction with the A28. Cross the road to **Hurst Close** opposite and follow it uphill to its very end, where it connects with a narrow footpath between gardens and by a brick wall. Turn left when this path terminates and go downhill alongside a line of conifer trees to a stile on the left. You may be surprised that this places you in a cemetery, but delighted, as I was, with its many benches. If you proceed downhill on the grass to meet the cemetery drive, you will approach an assembly of these benches at the bottom of the slope. Just the spot for a tea break (assuming you brought it with you!) while listening out for trains passing nearby. For a view of them you should go through the gap in the trees ahead.

5 While taking the usual precaution to 'stop, look and listen', you should go through that gap and over the railway. Having done that go forward and soon downhill through fields to a footbridge at the bottom. Soon turn right from the footbridge and walk to the far end

The 5.15pm arrives at Tenterden.

'Newenden' heads towards Tenterden and crosses our path.

of a very long tree-lined meadow. Crossing a footbridge there, climb the next meadow to the far right-hand corner, ignoring a gate on the right prior to the corner. A narrow path will then take you under trees and eventually to Tenterden station car park.

For the **Kent and East Sussex Railway** story, see page 66.

11
The Kent and East Sussex Railway – Wittersham Road to Northiam

4 miles

Taking the train from Northiam to Wittersham Road and walking back.

Useful maps: Ordnance Survey Explorer 125 or Landranger 188 and (for Northiam station) 189.

Hexden Channel.

The contrast between this and the previous walk could hardly be greater. It crosses a flat landscape of pastures and arable fields, intersected by numerous waterways and drainage ditches. Views of the railway are at first distant, which creates an atmosphere all of its own, especially as the sound of an engine radiates far and wide. Before you reach the one and only crossing of the railway, views are closer at hand. Beyond the railway, the path follows the attractive River Rother as far as Newenden, a delightful village with a cricket green, a church and a pub, and a fine stone-built bridge.

Getting there: By road: Northiam station is on the A28 ⅓ mile south of Newenden and 7 miles west of Rye – via the A268. It has a spacious car park, which is free to railway passengers. **Grid ref:** TQ835265 **Postcode:** TN31 6QT.

By public transport: Bus 2 from Hastings railway station to Tenterden calls at Northiam station 2-hourly, Tuesday to Saturday am, infrequently pm.

Eating out: Northiam station has its own refreshment room. At Newenden, which is ⅓ mile before the end of the walk, you will find the White Hart pub – which serves meals – and the Lime Wharf Café.

Visitor attractions: There are two local visits that you may wish to reserve for another day: the lovely gardens of **Great Dixter, Northiam**, and the National Trust's **Bodiam Castle**, which is a short walk from Bodiam station. Neither of these are on our walk.

The Walk

❶ Go left out of Wittersham Road station (at the level crossing) and walk with care along the road for 300 yards to a footpath on the left almost opposite **Maytham Farm**. Walk a succession of two fields at right angles to the road (110 degrees), crossing a footbridge at the half-way point. Aim for a gap in the trees ahead, and once there, turn sharp right at a crossing into a bridleway. The bridleway follows a ditch on the right and curves round to the right after 100 yards or so. It soon curves back to the left and in due course meets a road, the one we left earlier.

❷ Turn left at the road and almost immediately right into a wide farm track, which leads to **Maytham Wharf**, a farm. Ignore a branch on the left by a postbox, and veer right between farm buildings. Cross a wide waterway, **Hexden Channel**, soon after leaving the farm, and continue forward. The right of way is now on the grass alongside the right-hand wire fence, although the farm track runs more or less parallel and meets up at the next gate. If your timing is right you may have sight and sound of a steam engine as it passes well over to your right. You will be glad of those binoculars, or that telephoto lens on your camera! But in any case, you should have a closer view later on.

❸ The track follows a left-hand water channel and describes an S-bend before it comes within close range of the tree-shaded **New Barn**

Farmhouse. When you are just 50 yards from the farmhouse you should cross a ditch (at a gate) and turn right immediately to follow the ditch. Soon enter a large pasture and continue forward, following a slight left-hand curve in the ditch at the start. Now the order of the day is to take care, so that you avoid arriving at an impassable ditch – as I once did! Pass to the right of a band of trees that bisects the field ¼ mile ahead and soon enter the right-hand field but following a left-hand ditch. This ditch curves round to the right and escorts you to a crossing of the railway at **'Rother Bridge North'**.

❹ Now relax; and (hopefully again) watch a passing train. Beyond the crossing it's simply a matter of following the **River Rother** for one mile to **Newenden**. Before joining the A28 there, you will need to walk alongside the cricket green, passing to the left of the pavilion as you go. You may however wish to rest awhile before proceeding; or to visit either the **White Hart** to your right, or the **Lime Wharf Café** over the river to your left.

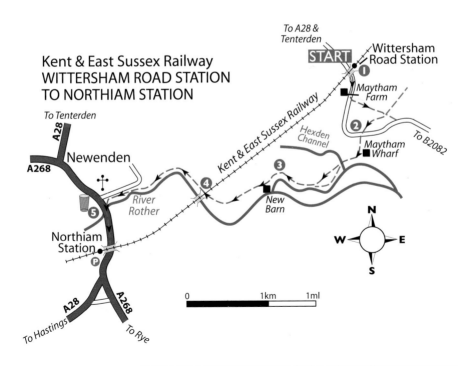

Kent & East Sussex Railway
WITTERSHAM ROAD STATION
TO NORTHIAM STATION

The river Rother at Newenden.

5 Refreshed and re-energised, and having crossed with great care the magnificent stone-built bridge over the River Rother, immediately join **Ferry Way**, a roadside path on the right. This will take you all the way back to Northiam station.

The Kent and East Sussex Railway story

With its 22 miles and 12 stations, the Rother Valley Railway came into being in the year 1900. Soon re-named the Kent and East Sussex Railway, it was built by the legendary Colonel H. F. Stephens, and was the first Light Railway in the world. Such railways conformed to the Light Railway Act of 1896, which allowed rural railways to be constructed economically with only basic passenger facilities and with weight and speed restrictions. The railway linked two main lines – from Headcorn on the London to Ashford line to Robertsbridge on the London to Hastings line.

After more than 50 years' service, the railway was closed to passengers in 1954. Twenty years later it reopened, in part, and as a volunteer-run heritage railway. By April 2000 it had reached Bodiam, close to the magnificent Bodiam Castle, which is now in the care of the National Trust.

Perhaps the railway was most fondly remembered for its conveyance of thousands of hop-pickers each year to the farms around Bodiam. For present-day travellers on the railway there is a unique opportunity to enjoy views of the countryside around the River Rother – views which only the railway can fully provide.

12
The Romney, Hythe and Dymchurch Railway, Kent

5 ½ miles

Taking the train from Hythe to Dymchurch and walking back.

Useful maps: Ordnance Survey Explorer 138 or Landranger 189.

Hythe, here we come!

From **Dymchurch the walk follows** the sea wall for 1 ¼ miles, enjoying magnificent sea views towards Dungeness to the south and Hythe and Folkestone to the north-east. It intercepts the railway on Romney Marsh and accompanies the track beyond Botolph's Bridge. The final ¾ mile is alongside the beautiful Royal Military Canal, terminating at Hythe station. Romney Marsh is not a wet place as you might suppose, but a well-drained agricultural area. However, you might welcome a compass as you cross it!

Railway operating days: Trains run every weekend throughout the year except in November, and daily from April to October inclusive; also a few days leading up to Christmas (except 25th and 26th) and the February school half-term. However, I cannot over-emphasise the value of having a timetable in-hand before setting out. This is available from The RH&DR, New Romney Station, New Romney, Kent, TN28 8PL. ☎ 01797 362353 ⊕ www.rhdr.org.uk

Getting there: By road: Hythe station is 5 miles west of Folkestone just off the A259. The station has a large car park for intending passengers. Roadside parking is also possible nearby. **Grid ref:** TR153348 **Postcode:** CT21 6LD.

By public transport: Bus routes 16,10 and 102 connect Folkestone's bus station to Hythe station and Dymchurch frequently every day. The bus station is a 15-minute walk from Folkestone Central railway station (trains from London Charing Cross or St Pancras International – the latter for a premium fare). Turn right out of the station, right under the railway bridge and left into Cheriton Road followed by Cheriton Gardens. The bus station is straight on.

Eating out: In Hythe's town centre there are a number of pubs and restaurants. The Vintage Style Tea Room sounds interesting and could be worth trying. In Dymchurch there is the Corner House Tea Rooms and Restaurant and the Ocean Inn; also Dymchurch Fish Bar – to name but a few. The Botolph's Bridge Inn is located 2/3 of the way along the walk.

Visitor attractions: Along with **Hastings, Romney, Dover** and **Sandwich, Hythe** is one of the ancient Cinque Ports, and received its charter back in 1278. It is well-worth exploring for its wealth of old houses, inns and shops. The **High Street** is just a ten-minute walk from the station. The station itself has a well-stocked gift shop. **Dymchurch** has been described as the **'Children's Paradise'**. That says quite a lot, you will agree!

The Walk

❶ From Dymchurch station go along **Station Road** and turn left at the road junction; then keep right at the next junction and head for the village centre. At the roundabout there turn left – the Hythe direction – and soon bear right at the traffic lights for the sea front. Following the same general direction, get onto the sea wall and stay with this for

1¼ miles, enjoying magnificent views – and the sea air – as you go. Looking forward along the coast you should have **Folkestone** in view, and looking back, the towers of **Dungeness nuclear power station**, which is beyond the extremity of the railway.

2 After passing a **Martello tower**, leave the sea wall by descending the second flight of steps to the road. That tower is one of many built along the coast from 1805 onwards as artillery stations to combat possible invasion from France. Keep right and cross the road to a short footpath immediately to the left of a **Jehovah's Witnesses Kingdom Hall**. Go along the path and turn right at the end into **Tower Estate**, and very soon turn left into a farm drive. An alternative route to this point passes to the right of the church. Passing between a farmhouse and the barns, go through a farm gate and into a paddock. Keep

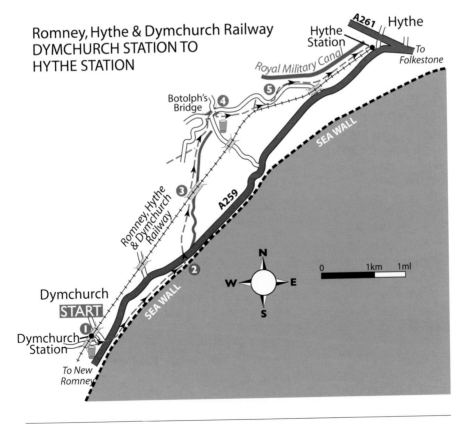

Romney, Hythe & Dymchurch Railway
DYMCHURCH STATION TO
HYTHE STATION

Rails across Romney Marsh.

forward again for 200 yards and leave the paddock at a pedestrian gate and footbridge in a corner on the right, and enter a pasture. You should walk across the pasture at an angle of about 20 degrees. (you will be glad you brought that compass, if indeed you did!).This should connect you with a stile and gate on the far side. Keeping straight on across the next pasture you will meet the railway in the far right-hand corner, by a drainage channel and to the right of a sewage farm. Spare a moment to look at the timetable (assuming you brought that with you also!) to see if a train is due.

3 Beyond the railway you have a long sequence of gates, stiles and footbridges taking you more or less straight on for one mile, mostly accompanied by a drainage channel, which is a little over to your right. After crossing the final footbridge a large bungalow will come into view ahead. You should pass to the left of the bungalow and enter a field on the right just beyond it. You can then connect with a road from the field's far left-hand corner.

4 Turn right in the road and, passing **Botolph's Bridge Inn**, cross the river bridge and immediately enter a field on the right. Keep over to the left there, walking parallel with the road and hopefully enjoying the view of a passing train. Go straight on for a few hundred yards; and when the road turns left (it is partly hidden by trees), go over one of two footbridges and soon bear left to follow the railway.

5 When a recreation ground appears on the left, cross it from a footbridge and turn right in a road from the opposite side. Leave the road when it turns right and go right yourself, but along the delightful **Royal Military Canal**. This canal extends over a distance of 28 miles from the sea near Folkestone to Cliff End in East Sussex. It was dug in the early 1800s as a defensive measure against the threat of invasion from France. Today the canal is vital in protecting Romney Marsh from drought in the summer and flooding in winter.

On arrival at a footbridge, you will see a miniature version of a 1930s acoustic dish, where a whisper on one side of the canal can be heard on the other. The full size versions were up to 200 metres in width, and were used to detect the sound of potentially offensive aircraft approaching the coast. These had limited use in the Second World War and were soon overtaken by the invention of radar, with its vastly improved range of detection.

The Royal Military Canal.

'Hercules' crosses the crossing at Dymchurch!

Leaving the footbridge behind (don't cross it), keep straight on with the canal. You will soon be accompanied by the railway, revealing its presence through gaps in the trees. Next stop Hythe station.

The Romney, Hythe and Dymchurch Railway story

This unusual 15-inch narrow-gauge railway was the brainchild of two 1920s racing drivers. These enthusiasts commissioned the construction of two narrow-gauge steam locomotives and hoped to develop a railway on which to operate them. With the unfortunate death in a racing accident of one of these founders, the remaining partner enlisted help in finding a suitable location. Romney Marsh was suggested and subsequently adopted. The railway opened from Hythe to New Romney in 1927 and was extended to Dungeness in 1928. In view of its potentially strategic position along the south-east coast of England it was requisitioned for war work in the 1940s. Photographs exist which show a heavily armoured military train on the railway.

When peace came the line was reopened to the public – with Laurel and Hardy cutting the ribbon for the final stage! Today the 13½ miles offer a spectrum of interest and delight: the Romney Marsh Visitor Centre accessible from Romney Warren Halt; Dungeness nuclear power station beyond the railway's terminal; and the railway HQ at New Romney with its gift shop, children's playground, model railway, buffet and Visitor Centre. Added to all this are the magnificent views across sea and shore. The railway also performs a very utilitarian function: carrying children daily to school and back.

13
Chinnor and Princes Risborough Railway
4½ miles

Taking the train from Chinnor to Princes Risborough and walking back.

Useful maps: Ordnance Survey Explorer 181 or Landranger 165.

The 'Watlington Flyer' at Chinnor.

With three railway lines fanning out from Princes Risborough, it's not surprising that our walk passes under a number of railway bridges near the start. With these behind us, we are soon at Horsenden, with its attractive and secluded church, before launching out across fields to the lovely village of Bledlow. The Three Lions pub at Bledlow presents an opportunity to rest awhile before continuing with the walk. The impressive heights of Wain Hill are over to the left, with the lowlands beyond the railway over to the right. Descending to Chinnor at the termination of a long chalky path, we soon cross the railway and meet Station Road and the station itself.

Railway operating days: Trains run every Sunday from April until October, and on December weekends (Saturdays and Sundays) leading up to Christmas. There are occasional Saturday and evening runs during the summer months. A timetable is available from Chinnor Station, Kiln Avenue, OX39 4ER; ☎ 07979 055366 (10am to 4pm); ⊕ enquiries@chinnorrailway.co.uk

Getting there: Chinnor Station is in Station Road, Chinnor and is signposted from the B4009 between Watlington and Princes Risborough. **Grid ref:** SP757004 **Postcode:** OX39 4BZ. It has a good car park which is free to intending passengers.

Eating out: Light refreshments are available on operating days from the Cambrian Coach Tea Room at Chinnor station. The village is well supplied with pubs along with a community café. And there is a general store for ice cream etc.

Visitor attractions: Chinnor station is a delight in itself, with the atmosphere of a country station in every respect. The beautifully kept carriages, signal box, platforms and station building are a credit to the volunteers who work so hard throughout the year. The **Church of St Andrew** is nearby – a complete contrast to the station, and where you can enjoy a few moments of quiet contemplation.

The Walk

❶ On leaving the train from **Princes Risborough's platform 4**, cross the railway by the footbridge. Go left on leaving the station, then soon right. Turn left at the far end of this road into **Summersley Road**. After passing under two railway bridges, take the second road on the left. This is signposted to the **Prince's Estate** and passes under yet another railway bridge. At the far end of this industrial estate keep forward through a gate and along a path between fields. After crossing a concrete farmyard turn right into a road by the entrance to **Horsenden Manor** and the delightful **Gate Cottage**. You will glimpse **Horsenden church** through the trees on the left, and its entrance gate where the road turns right.

❷ Continue forward, but now in a field, soon exiting the field at its opposite side. On entering another field keep forward again, passing to the left of a tall pylon. A hedge and ditch will accompany you along another, longer, field, and an exit will place you under a narrow band of trees. Turn left there and follow a path under the trees, but for 50 yards only. Leave the trees at that point and enter the field on the right, at a corner. Go along the left-hand edge of this and the next field and keep straight on along a drive, passing **Plum Tree Cottage** as you go. Turn left into the road at the far end, then right into **Church End, Bledlow**. If you have time to spare, do visit the **Lyde Garden** on the right. You will find it most pleasant and refreshing.

❸ On passing the **Lions of Bledlow** pub where the road turns right, keep forward across fields. You will meet a flinty track at the far end taking you forward. Leave the track after about 400 yards for a path on the right adjacent to a field corner. The railway will have come into view on your right as you cross the field (260 degrees). A ½-mile level path then takes you forward and parallel with the railway, eventually passing between a large timber building and the garden of **Wainhill Farm**. Cross a stile beside a postbox, turn right, then soon left – after noting the fine **Wainhill railway halt** nearby.

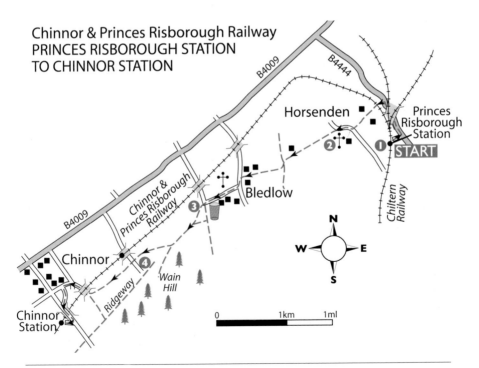

4 Stay with the path as it turns left, then right and runs parallel with the railway once again. Leave the path after ½ mile, then turn right into a track which comes down from the hills. You will soon enter **Chinnor village** with its general store and **Village Coffee Shop**, either of which you will doubtless find very welcome. Turn left by the store into **Church Road** and, passing **St Andrew's Church**, go first left into **Station Road**. Not surprisingly, Chinnor Station lies ahead.

Chinnor signal box.

The Chinnor and Princes Risborough Railway story

Laid down in 1872 and running from Princes Risborough to Watlington in Oxfordshire, this GWR branch line closed to passenger traffic in 1957, some years before Dr Beeching wielded his axe. All that remained in use was the section from Princes Risborough to Chinnor cement works for the conveyance of coal and gypsum; the former to power the furnaces, the latter for the cement manufacturing process. When the cement works closed down the railway became redundant. Soon on the scene came the 'Famous Five' of local railway enthusiasts, who met in the pub at Bledlow to discuss the possibility of keeping the railway open from Chinnor to Princes Risborough. The seed was sown at that meeting, and very soon the Chinnor and Princes Risborough Railway Association was born, and with only 30 members at the start. A valiant band of volunteers ensured that the railway went from strength to strength. The station building was constructed as an exact replica of the original; the signal box (moved here from Maidenhead) was craned in; and the platform was rebuilt.

In 1995 a saddle tank steam locomotive – 'Sir Robert Peel' – was purchased by the railway. Owing to technical problems with the locomotive, it was decided to sell her on; and that's after just 19 months service with the railway. Over subsequent years locomotives were taken on hire from other preserved railways.

For many years the railway terminated near Thame Junction (from where a branch once served Thame), but the ambition was to take it into Princes Risborough station. This it achieved – with a grand opening in 2018.

14
The Epping Ongar Railway, Essex

5 miles

Taking the train from North Weald to Ongar and walking back.

Useful maps: Ordnance Survey Explorer 183 or Landranger 167.

'Dinmore Manor' at Ongar Station.

After a very short stretch southward along the A128, we break free from Ongar's busy High Street and enter the lovely Essex countryside. Passing under the railway we follow a waterside path to the A414, soon leaving this for a good track and passing under

Railway operating days: Trains run on Saturdays and Sundays from April to October and at weekends leading up to Christmas. There are some Friday steamings in July and August; also at half-term school holidays. Timetables are available from Ongar Station, Station Approach, Ongar, Essex, CM5 9BN. ☎ 01277 365200 ⊕ enquiries@eorailway.co.uk

Getting there: By road: North Weald station is just off the B181, which connects with the A414, and beyond that the M11, Junction 7. **Grid ref:** TL496036 **Postcode:** CM16 6BT.
By public transport: The Central Line on London Underground terminates at Epping station where a heritage bus will take you to North Weald station. From there you can take the train to Ongar station for the start of the walk. The bus fare is included in the train fare.

Eating out: There is a buffet coach at North Weald station and a snack bar and picnic area at Ongar station.

Visitor attractions: Ongar station with its Grade II listing, is certainly an attraction in itself. Dating back to 1865, it has been restored by volunteers, and as such has received a National Railway Heritage Award.
Looking further afield, the beautiful **Greensted Church** is well worth a visit. The village lies south-west of Ongar, **Postcode:** CM5 9LD. The church is open daily from 10am.
Two and a half miles south of Ongar station – off the A128 – is the **Kelvedon ex-Nuclear Bunker**, which was built to house 600 personnel during the Cold War period, and is open to visitors. It even has a café – and is a good day out for families. **Postcode:** CM15 0LA.
North Weald Airfield can also be visited. It was established in 1916 and became an important air fighter station in the Second World War.

the railway again. The lovely settlement of Greensted Green with its beautiful pond is encountered before we cross fields again. We pass under the railway once more and follow a farm track before joining a footpath to North Weald station.

The Walk

1 From the station, turn right into **High Street**, then right again after about 300 yards by the supermarket. This will take you downhill and over a stream. Continue forward and uphill for about 50 yards, then turn right and follow a left-hand field edge. After the path curves round to the left, its route will take you over a footbridge and under a railway bridge. Turn left immediately beyond the bridge and follow a stream. This will lead you to the A414 road, where you should turn left.

2 Soon leave the road and join a track on the left that commences alongside a restaurant and runs between fields. It eventually crosses the railway (a good photo opportunity here) passes a pair of cottages and evolves into a footpath. Your path continues forward and joins a drive, which in turn enters **Greensted Green**.

3 Keep forward through the village along **Toot Hill Road**, with a beautiful pond over to your left. Where the road starts to descend, you should join a path on the right. This should cross the field half-left, but may be overgrown and not reinstated. Some walkers have obviously avoided this by following the right-hand field edge and have arrived at a railway bridge.

4 Join a field track that takes you under that bridge; then soon turn left. This takes you up through a farmstead and by a cottage (**Home View**). Turn left at the top in the direction of a radio mast and join a path on the right just prior to a railway bridge. Keep forward at

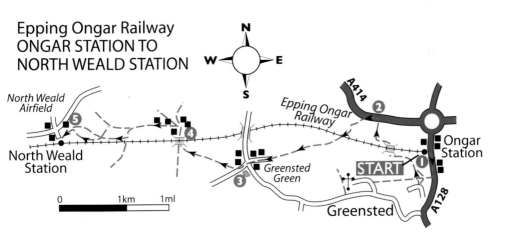

Epping Ongar Railway
ONGAR STATION TO
NORTH WEALD STATION

North Weald Airfield

North Weald Station

0   1km   1ml

Epping Ongar Railway

Greensted Green

Ongar Station

START

Greensted

a crossing and go alongside the railway or straight on, eventually along the left-hand edge of a sports field.

5 Go left from the field's far left-hand corner and straight on beside houses to **Station Road** to arrive at your destination.

The Epping Ongar Railway story

This Great Eastern Railway branch line appeared on the scene as far back as 1865. Following its time with the London North Eastern Railway, it operated under what we know as London Underground. Following their failed attempt to close the line in 1980, it continued until 1994, when it finally succumbed. It was sold on in 1998 and commenced its career as a preserved railway, enjoying its first run in 2004. After further closure – for essential restoration work – the line resumed operation in 2012.

The railway has enjoyed a number of accolades including the National Railway Heritage Volunteers' Award.

An intermediate station at Black Hall was closed in 1981 and is now in private ownership. With only around six passengers a day, its closure is no surprise.

Although 'Epping' is in the railway's title, the trains do not as yet use that station, but make a non-stopping about-turn nearby before returning to North Weald and Ongar.

London Underground Central Line trains terminate at Epping where heritage buses connect to North Weald station for the steam railway. Perhaps in the course of time it will commence at Epping station. That of course would deprive us of a fascinating ride on one of those ancient buses!